D1456696

Indians of the Amazon

There were probably around four million Amazon Indians before the arrival of Europeans at the beginning of the sixteenth century. In the succeeding years, the Indian population has been decimated by aggressive Portuguese settlers, epidemics of 'imported' diseases, greedy 'rubber barons' and, more recently, by land-grabbing speculators seeking to make the most of the Amazon basin's mineral wealth, timber and rich pasture-land. Today, there are under 100,000 Indians, whose future has become a very emotional issue. Should they be left to live as they have done for thousands of years or be integrated into modern society? The latter now seems inevitable, and it is hoped that it can be done without any further bloodshed. Marion Morrison has spent the last twenty years travelling all over the South American continent, frequently to very remote areas, while researching, writing and photographing. She has also written *Indians of the Andes* for this series.

Original Peoples

INDIANS
OF THE AMAZON

Marion Morrison

Original Peoples

Eskimos — The Inuit of the Arctic
Maoris of New Zealand
Aborigines of Australia
Plains Indians of North America
South Pacific Islanders
Indians of the Andes
Indians of the Amazon
Bushmen of the Kalahari
Pygmies of Central Africa
Bedouin — The Nomads of the Desert
The Zulus of South Africa

Frontispiece *A Yagua Indian man resting in his hammock.*

First published in 1985 by
Wayland (Publishers) Limited
49 Lansdowne Place, Hove
East Sussex BN3 1HF, England

© Copyright 1985 Wayland (Publishers) Limited

ISBN 0 85078 469 7

Phototypeset by Planagraphic Typesetters Limited
Printed in Italy by G. Canale & C.S.p.A., Turin
Bound in the U.K. by The Garden City Press
Limited, Herts.

Contents

Introduction

The Amazon of South America is the world's greatest river. Everything about it is vast. Rising in the snow-capped Andes 5,200 metres (17,000 feet) above sea-level, and just 193 km (120 miles) from the Pacific coast, it flows east for 6,400 km (4,000 miles) across the continent to the Atlantic Ocean. Such is its force that the fresh water penetrates the ocean 240 km (150 miles) out to sea, a fact first noticed by the Spanish sailor, Vincente Pinzon, who discovered the Amazon in 1500, and named it 'Fresh Water Sea'.

The mouth of the Amazon is over 320 km (200 miles) wide. With over 1,100 tributaries, the waters of the great river are said to make up 20 per cent of the world's fresh water, and drain an area almost the size of the USA. It is a region of tropical rain forest; huge trees with tangled lianas and large buttress roots; unfamiliar animals, like the tapir and capybara; and the home of a multitude of colourful birds and insects. Most of the rain forest lies in Brazil, but it also extends into eight of its neighbouring countries.

In 1541, Francisco Orellana, a Spanish soldier, led the first expedition down the Amazon. The journey took eighteen months and the men encountered many hazards on the way: rapids, starvation and hostile Indians — among them, it is said, the legendary tribe of women warriors, the Amazons, from whom the river took its name.

Beyond the river, in the dark forest, lived many more tribes of Indians who were only to encounter white men when Portuguese and Spanish colonists began to explore the interior. It was a tragic encounter for the Indians, whose numbers have since been reduced to a fraction of what they were at the time of the European conquest.

Left *A tributary of the Amazon slices through the thick tropical rain forest.*

VENEZUELA

GUYANA

SURINAM

FRENCH GUIANA

COLOMBIA

Makuna
Cubeo

Atroari

Island of Marajo

Manaus

R. Amazon

ro

Omagua

Mura

Kayapo

R. Purus

R. Xingu

BRAZIL

hipibo

Cintas Largas

Xingu
National
Park

PERU

Txukarramai

Caraja
Kreen-Akrore

Waura

Brasilia

BOLIVIA

Xavante

Yuracare

CHILE

PARAGUAY

ARGENTINA

Rio de Janeiro

Above *This map of South America shows the location of the tribes of Amazon Indians mentioned in this book.*

Left *The capybara is the largest rodent — one of the many unfamiliar animals to be found in the Amazon basin.*

7

Chapter 1 Discovery of the Indians

Origins and legends

Early man arrived in North America from Asia in the Ice Age, crossing the Bering Strait between Siberia and Alaska. He probably accompanied the migration of animals seeking new pastures and a warmer climate, and so made his way south some 10-20,000 years ago into the forests of South America.

Archaeology in the Amazon basin is difficult. Sites and artefacts are not easily found or preserved because of the frequent rainstorms, very humid climate and fast-growing vegetation. Also the early forest dwellers were nomadic hunters, moving from one place to another in search of game. They built temporary shelters of wood and thatch, materials that quickly decay in such conditions.

The most significant finds have been large natural mounds, formed by the accumulation of shells, which have been used as burial places and contain human remains, some crude stone hammers and fragments of pottery. These mounds are particularly evident on the Island of

Armadillos, like this one, are part of the Amazon Indian's diet. They are baked in their shells.

Marajo, an island the size of Switzerland that lies in the Amazon's mouth. Marajoara pottery is very fine and includes jars, bowls and figurines. From such scant evidence, archaeologists believe people were living in the Amazon basin by 3000 BC and have classified them into four main language groups: Je, Carib, Arawak and Tupi.

There are many Indian legends and myths which tell of their origins,

Like the early inhabitants of the Amazon's forest, many tribes are still nomadic hunters, like these Indians.

describing gods, jaguars behaving like men, fire devastating the earth, and twins, one good and one bad. Such stories, elaborated by time, are passed from Indian to son, generation by generation, around the evening family fire.

9

Time of conquest

The Portuguese Admiral, Pero Alvares Cabral, with a fleet of thirteen ships first sighted the coast of Brazil in April 1500. He was lucky in two ways. First, because he had been blown off course while on his way to India; and secondly, because the land he had discovered could be claimed by his own king. Following the discovery of America by Columbus in 1492, the Treaty of Tordesillas was signed in 1494. This divided the unknown world between Spain and Portugal, and the coast of Brazil fell

Admiral Cabral claims Brazil for Portugal, on 22 April 1500.

within the sphere of Portugal.

Cabral stayed only nine days on this visit, but he was accompanied by the chronicler Caminha who described their first meeting with the natives: 'they were dark and entirely naked, with nothing to cover their private parts, and carried bows and arrows in their hands.'

The Indians were expert hunters and fishermen. Using long bows of hard, dark wood and feathered arrows, they could kill with astonishing accuracy. They had no domestic animals and farmed only a few plants, like manioc and maize — a diet which they supplemented with

The Indians have always been expert marksmen with the bow and arrow.

wild honey, nuts, fruits and some edible grubs from the forest.

At first, the Portuguese were delighted with the friendly attitude of the natives, but they soon became aware of the aggressive Tupi Indians, who were constantly at war with the other tribes. The fighting and surprise attacks were often very cruel and dominated the native life on the coast. In time, the Portuguese were to learn that colonizing their new territory was not as simple as it seemed at first.

Chapter 2 **Disasters of colonization**

Barter to slavery

At first sight, there were no obvious riches in the new territory — no gold, silver or precious minerals. Instead the Portuguese were content to trade the magnificent great tree, the brazil wood, from which a red dye can be extracted which was then fashionable in Europe. The tree later gave its name to the country of Brazil. In return for helping to cut and load the giant logs, the Indians were delighted to receive their first metal axes and tools, as well as oddments of mirrors, combs and clothing.

Inevitably the coastal supply of brazil wood began to decline and so too did the Indians' interest in their newly acquired gifts. And when more, larger groups of settlers began to arrive on the 4,000 km (2,500

Few Indians willingly went to work on the European settlers' sugar plantations, as this picture of a slave army shows.

mile) long coast, they looked for a new industry. They found the mild climate ideal for growing sugar. But cutting cane, running the mills and boiling molasses involved hard labour that required a large body of men. The Indians, disinterested in acquiring more goods for which they had little use, were unwilling to cooperate, particularly in work which did not require their hunting skills.

The natives quickly became disenchanted with the Europeans. Not only did they resent slavery, but their women were being taken by the settlers, who clearly had come to stay. In the years that followed, the coastal communities suffered constant war as Indians resisted settlers; Indian fought Indian; and settlers defended the lands they had acquired. Some settlers made huge profits. Thousands of Indians died; while those who could, fled from the coast to seek refuge in the huge Amazon forest.

Sugar cane being harvested on a Brazilian plantation in the seventeenth century.

Plagues from Europe

At the time of discovery, it was generally reported that the Indians were of excellent health, living to a remarkable old age. Not only were there large populations of them living along the Atlantic coast, but as Francisco Orellana observed on his Amazon journey, there were numerous and very large villages along the river: 'the further we went, the more thickly populated and better did we find the land.'

But although the Indians seemed healthy enough, it quickly became apparent that they had no immunity to disease. After the European conquest, endless and widespread epidemics of fever, dysentery, influenza, measles, plague and smallpox took hundreds of thousands of lives. Entire communities and whole tribes of Indians were wiped out.

One group of missionaries did what they could to help the Indians. They were the Jesuits who had been sent to Brazil to convert the natives to Christianity. They set up large mission settlements, to which thousands of Indians flocked both for religious teaching and for protection from the coastal wars. The Jesuits offered the Indians some hope, particularly as they opposed slavery. But when the epidemics struck, despite incredible medical efforts by some missionaries, disease spread rapidly through Indian communities.

During the three hundred years of colonial rule, the Indians were the victims of the settlers' fight to survive and to profit; of the Church's desire to convert them to Christianity; and of devastating disease. Brazil

The Indians gained little from 300 years of Portuguese rule. Even if they survived 'imported' diseases, harsh treatment at the hands of their conquerors resulted in the death of many. And this was before rubber was discovered in the Amazon basin . . .

A view of Rio de Janeiro, the capital of Brazil until 1960. Discovered in 1502, the Portuguese were responsible for laying the foundations of this thriving port and industrial centre.

became an independent country in 1822, and slavery was officially abolished in 1888. But this did not protect the Indians when white man discovered rubber in the upper Amazon.

Left *This seventeenth-century figure of Christ was carved in wood by Guarani Indians, under the instruction of some Jesuit missionaries. As well as trying to convert them to Christianity, the Jesuits tried to improve the lot of the Indians under foreign rule.*

15

The Rubber Boom

People have been making use of the latex from rubber trees for hundreds of years. Columbus saw people on the Caribbean island of Haiti playing with rubber balls in 1495. Two hundred and fifty years later, the French scientist and explorer, de la Condamine found Omagua Indians in Ecuador using the rubber tree's latex to waterproof simple goods. But it was Charles Goodyear's discovery of vulcanization that turned the gummy liquid into a commercially viable product.

The demand for rubber lured entrepreneurs of many nationalities into the remotest Amazon tributaries. Wild rubber trees (the scientific name is *Hevea brasiliensis)* are scattered throughout the forest, though in certain regions they are more abundant and can yield more latex. The process of obtaining the latex is simple. Once the tree is found, the bark is slashed with a shallow cut and the latex oozes out, to be collected in small cups. Each day the liquid is gathered and formed into round balls by slowly dripping it on to a wooden spindle rotated in smoke.

Latex being collected by a worker on a Brazilian rubber plantation.

the boom, in 1910, that some of the scandalous acts of barbarism were brought to the world's attention by an American traveller, Walter Hardenburg. His personal campaign to expose the scandal coincided with the collapse of the Rubber Boom, but it was too late for the thousands of Indians who had died.

Below *Charles Goodyear, who discovered vulcanization.*

The famous Opera House in Manaus.

The gathering and smoking was the work of thousands of Indians enslaved by wealthy 'rubber barons', who kept private armies to enforce their control. With the wealth, cities were constructed containing extravagant buildings, like the famous Opera House in Manaus.

It was not until nearly the end of

Chapter 3 **Way of life**

Harvesting the Amazon

Forest Indians live by a combination of hunting, fishing, gathering wild produce and 'slash and burn' agriculture. The Indians fell trees and burn a clearing to form their field, or 'garden', for growing crops. Because Amazon soil is easily exhausted — heavy rain soon washes the nutrients away — the gardens have a short life, and the Indians move on every five years or so.

The Indians' staple crop is manioc, which in its natural state contains poisonous prussic acid. To remove it, the Indians use a *tipiti,* a cylindrical press made of vine. Washed manioc is put in the *tipiti* and squeezed to release the poison. The pulp is then dried, mixed into a paste with water and pressed into flat pancake-like 'loaves'. Other cultivated crops include maize, yams,

Txicao women (members of a tribe from the River Xingu region) harvesting manioc.

groundnuts and bananas. From the forest, Indians gather many other plants, fruits, berries, wild honey and spices, including peppers.

The Amazon teems with fish of all kinds. Even the piranha, or 'cannibal' fish, is good to eat. Some fish, like the *pirarucu,* grow to over 2.5 metres (8 feet) long; while catfish can weigh over 180 kilograms (400 lbs). Indians near rivers never go hungry and use a variety of bows, arrows, nets, traps and even poisons to catch fish.

Blowpipes are the traditional and most important weapon used by the

Txicao boys cut up a tapir which they have hunted and killed.

Indians for hunting. A small dart shot from a blowpipe can hit a target some 36 metres (120 feet) away. Sometimes the darts are tipped with curare, a poison which immobilizes climbing animals by causing them to relax their grip and fall to the ground. Fresh meat also comes from a variety of animals caught in traps and snares, or killed with spears and arrows. Wild pigs, rodents of all kinds and tapirs form part of the rich larder provided by the forest.

A well-stocked storehouse

Amazon Indians have never discovered metal and, in much of the enormous low-lying basin, stone is rare. But despite the lack of these materials, the Indians have perfected substitutes from the natural resources around them.

Arrows and spears, instead of

Men making traps to catch fish.

being tipped with metal, are carved with barbs or points made of immensely hard wood, like the *chonta* palm. The same wood is used for making nails to hold pieces of timber together. Alternatively, in places where such hard woods are scarce, the tribes use the bark of trees or lianas, cut into strips, to serve as thongs for binding.

Although they have little need for clothing, most Amazon tribes are expert weavers. Cotton (both wild and cultivated) is woven on looms into hammocks, slings and waistbands, and in some communities in the Andean foothills, into long poncho-like garments called *cushmas*. Cloth made from the bark of trees, stamped with painted designs, is used particularly among the Yuracare Indians. Other tribes weave strips of bark and wood into baskets or bowls. These may be waterproofed with gums from a variety of trees.

Fire is known over most of the Amazon basin, and food is baked, grilled or roasted. In places where there is good clay, pottery has been developed, and tribes like the Waura are renowned for their imaginative designs. Otherwise for cooking, tribes make use of a variety of containers from turtle shells to vegetable gourds. Animals, such as armadillos, can be baked in their shell.

For transport, the Indians have a variety of craft: simple rafts made of very light balsawood, dug-out canoes and canoes made of bark.

An Indian family enjoying a forest barbecue.

A forest home

Amazon Indian houses are traditionally simple, yet functional, and always built in harmony with the surrounding tropical forest. Made from wood and thatch, the dwellings reflect the nomadic life style of the Indians and are easily discarded when the tribes move on to a new location.

Designs and styles of houses relate to the needs of the people and their immediate environment. So the Caraja have rows of houses along the high banks of the Araguaia river; while the Mura Indians of the Madeira and Purus rivers use canoes which they convert into dwellings.

Housing also mirrors the economic organization and social structure of the families or village. Sometimes, a village can consist of several hundred individuals, but generally they are small, containing perhaps about fifty. A characteristic arrangement, as with the Kayapo Indians of central Brazil, are houses arranged around a square, behind which are huts where the women cook. In the middle of the square is one hut for the men, which can also

Over 2 metres (6½ feet) long, the arapaima is one of the largest fish in the River Amazon and its tributaries.

be used for ceremonial activities.

A feature of the north-west Amazon is the *maloca*. This is a huge communal building that can accommodate up to two hundred people. Inside there are no walls but space is allotted to each family. The construction of a *maloca* is very precise: each part has a symbolic meaning. Among the Makuna Indians, for example, the four central posts represent the mountains which support

An aerial view of a typical Indian village. Made from wood and thatch, its houses are simple, but functional.

the heavens; the ridge at the top marks the limit of the universe; and the circular floor, the earth. There is little furniture, the Indians sleeping on mats or on platform beds, though hammocks are now found all over the Amazon.

Tribal society

Inside Indian houses, each family has its own fireplace where everyone gets together to eat or discuss the day's events. Families are large by Western standards, often taking in distant relatives. A happy family unit is fundamental to Indian life and essential for survival. Members of the family are very dependent on each other and content to be so.

Men and women have their allotted tasks, so while men clear and prepare gardens, women do the planting and harvesting. Women cook inside the hut, but 'forest meals' are prepared by the men. Men never carry water — that is women's work, even on long marches through the forest.

In this relaxed atmosphere children grow up surrounded by love and the attention of all the family. They learn the skills of their tribes, not by instruction, but by watching and imitating.

Puberty, or coming-of-age, is an important event in tribal life and celebrated with elaborate festivities. For the children, it can be a painful process: boys are sometimes whipped or subjected to the stings of hornets or poisonous ants. Girls sometimes have their hair shaved or pulled out (the new growth symbolizing the emergence of an adult personality), and often they are kept apart from the rest of the tribe, secluded in a hut for several months. But the children undergo these initiation ceremonies without complaint or fear, as they accept adulthood and early marriage as part of their responsibilities towards their tribe.

A happy family unit is essential for survival in the tropical forest.

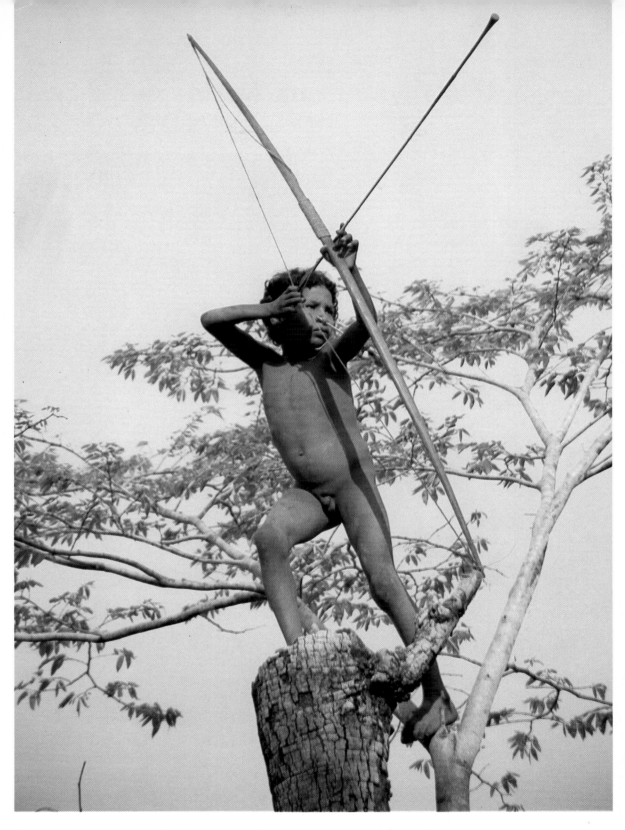

Children learn the skills of their tribes by watching and imitating.

Chapter 4 **A mysterious world**

Indian art

Ceremonial and magical practices play an important part in the life of an Amazon Indian. There are festivals related to the sun and moon, the seasons, the fertility of plants, birth and, especially, death. All symbolize the Indian belief in

Men playing sacred flutes.

Chief Raoni of the Txukarramai Indians.

spirits and the supernatural, as seen around them in the forest.

At times of festivals, men and women work hard to make their bodies beautiful. Indians love to paint themselves: some because they otherwise feel naked; men and women to make themselves attractive to the opposite sex; mothers paint babies to send them to sleep. Applying the paint, made from natural

26

dyes, is a group activity and part of the fun of dressing up.

But for special occasions, everyone indulges in elaborate adornments. Almost all the ornaments come from nature: necklaces, ear-plugs and nose-pieces of shell, bones and animals' teeth; exquisite multi-coloured bands and crowns of feathers from macaws, parrots and toucans; sweet-smelling tree saps and pungent fruit oils. One tribe, the Cubeo, is famous for its bark-cloth masks representing spirits

Indians love to decorate themselves.

Bird feathers make a splendid hat!

and demons, and worn to ward off evil powers at funeral ceremonies.

Amazon Indians play pan-pipes and flutes made from animal bones or bamboo, drums from animal skins, maracas carved out of gourds, and rattles of nutshells. One special flute is used by some tribes in the Xingu river region. It is nearly 1.2 metres (4 feet) long, made of wood and emits a deep booming noise like a horn. This flute is believed to be the symbol and voice of a spirit, and must never be seen by women.

27

Jungle magic

Jungle Indians believe spirits control many aspects of their life, like good health and a good harvest. So they must take care to keep peace with these spirits, which they do through the *shaman*. Any man in a tribe can become a *shaman* if he feels a call to do so, and if he is prepared to undergo certain rigorous and frightening ceremonies.

The *shaman* is important to the tribe. He may use his powers to avert storms; to bring success in hunting; or to ward off hostile spirits sent by other tribes. Or he can send out his own spirits to cause damage and disaster to enemies. His social duty is to cure the sick, and he must employ the right spirit to help him. So the 'fish spirit' may be called down to

A dance to celebrate a successful manioc harvest.

28

because of their controlled use, it has been observed that the Indians seem not to suffer ill-effects.

Once the drug begins to take effect, the *shaman* chants and dances. He appears to be in another world, waving his arms in the air and stamping his feet, his postures reflecting the personality of the spirit he has chosen to help him. As the effects of the drug wear off, he stops, exhausted and returns to the normal world in an instant, as if nothing has happened.

Below *Quinine bark, which is used by the Indians to cure malaria, eye infections and upset stomachs.*

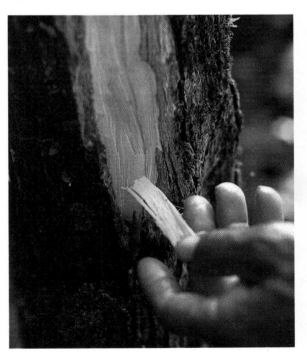

spray water over a patient and so lower his temperature; while the spirits of monkeys, said to have 'sticky hands', are used to extract a disease from a patient's body.

To assist him in his work, the *shaman* uses special medicinal plants from the forest. Leaves from the jacaranda tree are applied to a snakebite; while quinine, from the cinchona tree, is used against malaria, eye infections and upset stomachs. Some native drugs which produce hallucinations, or visions, can be used only by the *shaman*. The *shaman* practises several times each week with these special drugs, and

Chapter 5 **Into the twentieth century**

Amazon under threat

'Die if need be, never kill' was the slogan of the great Brazilian explorer, Rondon, himself part-Indian. He headed the Indian Protection Service (SPI) which was set up in Brazil in 1910 in the wake of the atrocities of the Rubber Boom.

The problems facing the SPI were immense. Amazon Indians still occupied vast, unknown territories. Some, who had made contact with

Busy, bustling Manaus — once the rubber capital of the world.

whites, had acquired rifles to defend themselves. Most important, the so-called Indian problem developed into a straightforward dispute over land when the significance of the Amazon basin was suddenly appreciated as a source of mineral wealth, oil, valuable wood and lush pasture.

The right of the Indian to the land on which he lives, though supported by laws going back to colonial times, has never been enforceable in practice. As a result, and ignoring the Indian presence, vast areas of land were sold to speculators in Brazil, Europe and America. In turn, the development of the land was only achieved at the expense of the Indian, thousands of whom were systematically exterminated by well-armed expeditions. There were instances of poisoned food, clothing infected with a smallpox virus and at least one incident in which Indian villages were bombed from the air. Once an area was cleared of Indians, then the huge farming combines, landless settlers, and gold prospectors took over.

Much of this was carried out with the agreement and knowledge of SPI workers. In 1968 the organization was disbanded in the middle of a great scandal. It was replaced by the National Indian Foundation (FUNAI).

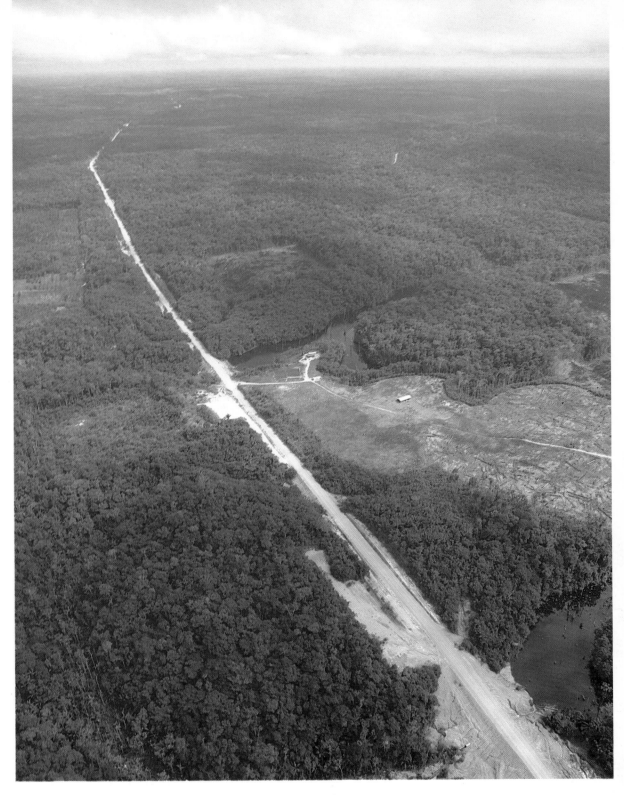

Nothing stands in the way of the Amazon highway as it cuts through the forest.

Xingu: an Indian reservation

In the early 1940s, Orlando Villas Boas and his brothers, Claudio and Leonardo, were in the central Amazon on a government mission to open up land for development. They soon realized that their work, however well-intentioned, meant disaster for the many Indians they met, and they decided to do something about it.

The brothers planned a reservation where the Indians would be encouraged to work and live as they always had, without having to make

Above *Claudio Villas Boas helped set up the Xingu National Park.*

Below *Body-painting is an essential part of daily life for this Xingu woman.*

Room for one more? A Txicao village moving to the Xingu National Park.

a hurried choice between their culture and that of modern Brazil. In 1961, with the help of FUNAI, the brothers created a national park. The area chosen was around the Xingu river, a region poor in mineral wealth, relatively difficult to get to and to which several tribes had already retreated in the face of the white man's invasions.

Today nearly 2,000 members of 14 tribal societies live in the park. They come from several different racial origins and each tribe still speaks its own language and preserves many of its own myths and characteristics.

However, through contact with each other over a long period, the tribes have developed some similar customs. Villages are broadly the same, with palm-thatched communal huts in a circle, and gardens of manioc and maize nearby.

Medical posts are run with the help of volunteers, and an airstrip has been built by each village so that the sick can be flown to the small hospital. The Indians are vaccinated against smallpox and measles, as there have been several epidemics. As a result, the number of Indians in the park has increased.

Xingu: success or failure?

Some years ago, one visitor to the park wrote that 'the remarkable thing about the Xingu is that it works.' But the question has to be asked: for how long?

In 1971, the Brazilian government announced a gigantic Trans-Amazonica road-building campaign, designed to open up the interior. Highway BR80, originally planned to go round the north end of the park, was suddenly diverted to run right through it, completely disrupting the villages of the Txukarramai Indians. There was no apparent reason for this sudden change of plan, and the Villas Boas brothers were not consulted.

Then, after the highway was completed, a vast expanse of land north of the road, originally in the park, was put on sale. Again the Txukarramai Indians were disturbed and they reacted violently by killing a

Xingu Indian chiefs discuss land problems with representatives from FUNAI.

A wrestling contest taking place in a Xingu village.

number of white workers on local *fazendas* (farms). Although a compromise was reached over the land, the incident could well prove to be a landmark in the history of the Xingu.

The Villas Boas brothers felt obliged to resign from FUNAI and left the Xingu. (Leonardo died in 1962.) Despite thirty years of dedicated work, they have seen their original concept of keeping the Indians in isolation, eroded by the tribes' contact with white settlers.

Often this contact surfaces in the more harmful aspects of civilization: drink, prostitution and violence. Many Indians now understand that money or trading goods can buy small luxuries, like transistor radios, and will try to get work on nearby farms in return for pay. Most important, perhaps, is the Indians' realization that in order to survive, they have to retain the land which the government says is legally theirs. And for this, they have shown that they are prepared to kill.

Uncontacted tribes

Remarkably, there are still unknown tribes hidden in the Amazon forest. In recent years, as highways have penetrated deeper into the forest, there has been an even more urgent need to contact them.

In 1968, FUNAI sent three parties to 'pacify' three warlike tribes. One team went to the Atroari in the north, and although virtually the entire party was wiped out, a follow-up expedition made peace. The second group went to the Cintas Largas in the west, where they had to wait in the jungle for almost two years, eventually persuading some of the tribe to come out of hiding. The third expedition, under the leadership of the Villas Boas brothers, went in search of the Kreen-Akrore.

One of the first signs that this unknown tribe existed came when a young British scientist was attacked and killed in an area where no Indians were thought to live. Then the long-haired Txukarramai captured a small boy from a tribe they called the 'people with short hair', the Kreen-Akrore.

The Villas Boas brothers first set

Presents being left to encourage the Kreen-Akrore to come out of hiding in the forest.

out by air to locate Kreen-Akrore houses. Rudely constructed of banana leaves, they are difficult to detect through the dense cover of jungle trees, but one village was sighted. Later, after struggling upriver for several months, a second Villas Boas expedition reached the village. It was deserted. As is the custom, gifts of mirrors, knives, steel axes and toys for the children were left hanging on trees. The Kreen-Akrore returned to the village, unseen, and took the gifts.

This 'hide and seek' procedure was maintained, and after many expeditions and frustrations lasting five years, contact was at last made. The Kreen-Akrore were persuaded to move into the Xingu Park. But the story does not have a happy ending. One report claims that of the original 140 members of the tribe, 66 have died from disease.

First contact with members of the Kreen-Akrore.

Chapter 6 **Today and tomorrow**

Headhunters of the Amazon

The Jivaro Indians live on the border of Peru and Ecuador, where the Amazon lowlands meet the jungle-covered eastern slopes of the Andes mountains. They have long been considered one of the most hostile groups in the Amazon, a reputation based on their practice of shrinking the heads of their enemies. In the old Jivaro culture, this custom was closely bound up with a complicated mythology of the soul, whereby a man could become strong and powerful.

With the arrival of the twentieth century and the opening up of the Amazon, many things have changed and the Jivaro no longer shrink heads. The tribe developed contact with white civilization when the area in which it lives became part of a colonization programme, started by the Ecuadorian government. The region is vast, very rich in resources, but had remained virtually unexplored for centuries.

The colonization programme failed because the highland people, who tried to work there, could not adjust to different methods of farming, a very humid climate and a poor soil. They abandoned the experiment, leaving behind a network of roads and landing strips.

Meanwhile a group of the Jivaro, the Shuar, had learned enough to set up their own organization to fight for their rights. They created the *Federacion de Centros Shuar* in 1965. The organization now has a membership of 20,000 and many achievements to its credit: notably

The Jivaro Indians have always been considered a hostile tribe because of their practice of shrinking the heads of their enemies, like this one.

the survey and registration of their tribal lands as collective property, and a successful radio school system. This unique project comprises 100 radio schools relaying bilingual lessons to some 2,000 pupils, including children in very remote areas. The programmes are especially designed to take in the social and cultural background of the Indians.

A Jivaro woman preparing some food. Note the metal cooking pots in the background.

Adopting Western ways

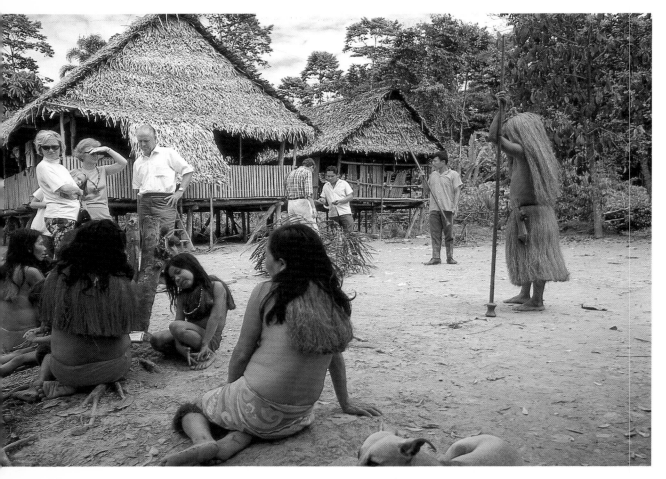

Western tourists visiting a Yagua village.

Some groups of Indians have already learned to live with modern civilization, though the extent of this 'integration', as it is called, depends on the circumstances of the tribe.

In the upper tributaries of the Peruvian Amazon are tribes of Indians who were first contacted by missionaries during colonial times, and who then found themselves in the centre of the rubber boom. For the first time, in the twentieth cen-

tury, they have been faced with making their own judgement on modern civilization.

Some have integrated completely, such as the descendants of the Cocama tribe who now live like rural Peruvians. A generation ago the women still wore traditional dress, but this has been rejected in favour of Western-style clothing. The group now speaks Spanish, lives in towns, and appears embarrassed if reference is made to their Indian background.

Their neighbours, the Shipibo, have reacted differently. While accepting some aspects of western civilization, they have retained many of their Indians traditions. The women wear traditional skirts of hand-woven cotton, with Western-style blouses. The men have Western clothes but put on traditional *cushmas* for fiestas. Though nominally Catholic, they still celebrate some Indian festivals, in

Many Indians are rejecting traditional dress for Western-style clothing.

particular puberty rights for young girls. The Shipibo have always been known for highly decorated pottery and cloth, which they still make and sell to tourists.

One aspect of their tribal life, though, will probably determine their future. The Shipibo are essentially fishermen and where they live is dictated by the availability of fish. As the people in towns and communities rapidly consume catches from nearby rivers, the Shipibo are being forced to settle in remoter areas, where there are few educational or medical facilities.

Voice in government

It is a sad fact that, while the remaining Amazon Indians are upheld as survivors of an ancient culture on the one hand, their position as underdog is frequently taken for granted. Even today, their society and the innocent nature of the Indian is sorely abused. One problem is that, without education, the Indian may never attain a position of authority in the central governments of South America. People of mixed blood have occasionally achieved recognition as writers or artists, but for a pure Indian, a voice in government is almost unknown.

An exception is Mario Juruna, a Xavante Indian from the Mato Grosso (between the River Araguaia and River das Mortes) in Brazil. He first gained the attention of government authorities in 1974 when he led his tribe in a campaign against 'landowners' who were encroaching on tribal territory. Bit by bit and with the gradual changes of the political climate, Mario Juruna found himself nationally famous, and was eventually elected in 1983 to the position of 'Deputy' for the State of Rio de Janeiro, as a member of one of the opposition parties.

Juruna has learned Portuguese and with his young wife, Doralice, spends much of his time in Rio de Janeiro. He is a popular figure, respected for his traditional Indian honesty, and people stop his car in the street to ask for his autograph. He has adopted Western dress, and takes part in many TV debates and

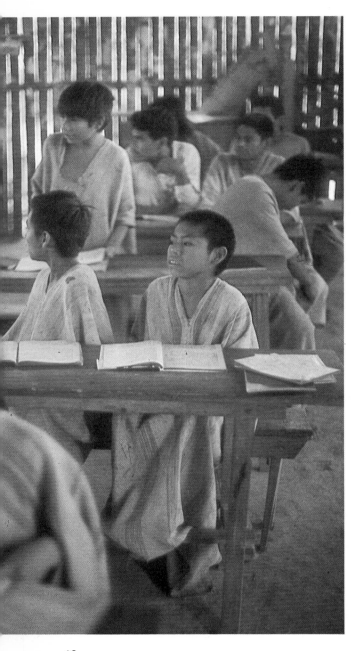

Left *Indian children being taught at a missionary school.*

chat-shows.

Being an elected Deputy, Juruna is able to travel extensively and make use of modern communications for his campaigns. But more important, he has a vote in the Brazilian government. And although his is only one voice, he has already been able to rally support for Indian causes, especially land disputes.

Shipibo women selling some of their handiwork.

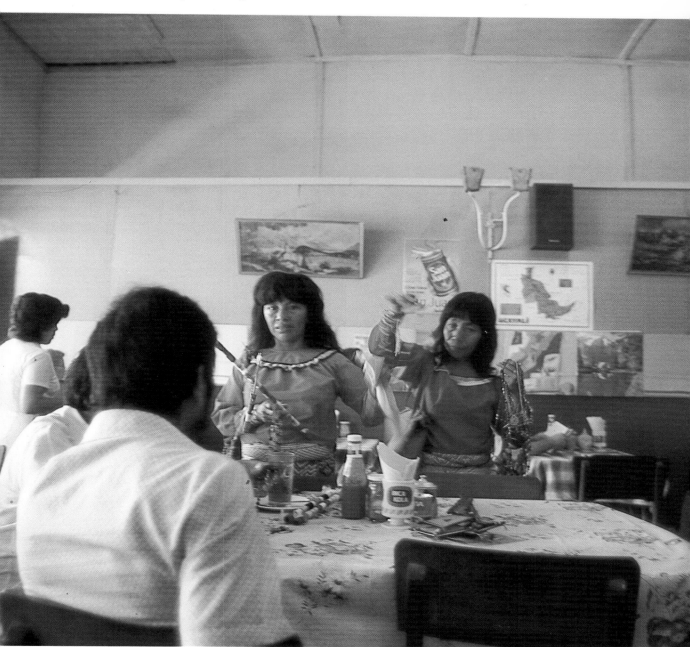

The future

Estimates of the number of Indians living in Brazil are at best guesswork. The original population has been variously recorded as between 2 and 6 million. Of the 230 tribes in existence at the turn of this century, 87 are said to have disappeared by 1968. Today, with no greater degree of certainty, the total number of Indians could be less than 100,000: a very small minority when compared with Brazil's total population of 125 million.

To accommodate so many people, there is an increasing need to open up the interior and develop industries. But with each new highway and the destruction of the surrounding forest, the world of the last few Indians is threatened.

The future of the Indians is a very emotional issue in South America.

An Indian boy being injected against a 'Western' disease.

Huge chunks of the Amazon rain forest are being cleared for housing developments.

Should they be left to live as they have done for many centuries? Or should they be integrated into modern society? There are people who oppose the Villas Boas brothers' policy of isolation. They argue that the Indians already demand tractors, schools, and medical assistance, and that they want to help build their country.

The Villas Boas brothers would reply by asking into what can the Indians be integrated? They believe this integration would mean the Indians living at the lowest level of society, in the slums of the big cities, their culture and traditions having been completely lost.

And what do the Indians feel? This is the most difficult question to answer. To step from a Stone Age culture into the technical age of the twentieth century is a daunting prospect. But the hope must be that improved medical attention and education will help the Indians to cope with the integration which now seems inevitable, and which they seem to want. But for the moment, as Claudio Villas Boas has observed: 'by saving his life, you do not solve the Indian problem, you just preserve the Indian to have a problem about.'

Glossary

Artefacts   The items of ancient civilizations, found by archaeologists.

Blowpipe   A hunting weapon made of hard wood, from which small, poisonous darts are blown.

Brazil wood   A tree valued for its red dye.

Capybara   The world's largest rodent, which lives in Amazon forests.

Chronicler   A person who provides a contemporary account of events.

Hallucination   Seeing something that is not there: an illusion.

Immunity   Having resistance to disease.

Initiation   A beginning. As in initiation ceremonies, when young Indian boys and girls 'begin' their adult life.

Integration   The mixing together of two races of people.

Jesuits   The Catholic missionaries (see below). An Order founded by Ignatius Loyola in 1533.

Latex   The sap of the rubber tree.

Malaria   A fever caused by the bite of a mosquito.

Missionaries   The people sent to another country to convert the natives to Christianity.

Molasses   A treacle-like substance produced in the refining of sugar.

Nomadic   A way of life in which people have no fixed home, but move on from one place to another.

Quinine   A bitter-tasting extract of the *cinchona* tree bark, used to suppress malaria.

Reservation   An area of land which is protected for the exclusive use of native tribes.

Speculator   A person who takes a risk in investing in land or other business enterprises.

Tambours   A drum, especially a bass drum.

Tapir   The largest land mammal in the Amazon.

Vulcanization   The industrial process in which rubber is treated with sulphur, at high temperatures, to provide a strong and flexible material.

Books to read

Collier, Richard *The River that God Forgot* (Collins, 1968)

Cowell, Adrian *The Heart of the Forest* (Gollancz, 1960)

Cowell, Adrian *The Tribe that Hides from Man* (Bodley Head, 1973)

Furneaux, Robin *The Amazon* (Hamish Hamilton, 1971)

Hanbury-Tenison, Robin *Aborigines of the Amazon Rain Forest: The Yanomami* (Time-Life Books)

Hemming, John *Red Gold* (Macmillan, 1978)

Henley, Paul *Amazon Indians* (Macdonald Educational, 1980)

Hugh-Jones, Stephen *A Closer Look at Amazon Indians* (Hamish Hamilton, 1978)

Lathrap, Donald W. *The Upper Amazon* (Thames and Hudson, 1970)

Man, John *Jungle Nomads of Ecuador: The Waorani* (Time-Life Books)

McConnell, Rosemary *The Amazon* (Wayland, 1978)

Peoples of the Earth: Amazonia & Pampas (The Danbury Press, New York)

Glossary of Indian, Spanish and Portuguese words

Chonta (pronounced *chon tar*) A palm that supplies both food and hard woods for bows.

Curare *(coo rah ray)* A deadly poison used on blowpipe darts to immobilize or kill.

Cushma *(coosh marh)* A long hand-woven cotton poncho mainly worn by Amazon tribes living near the Andean foothills.

Fazenda *(fa shen dar)* An estate, farm or ranch in Brazil.

FUNAI *(foon aiy)* The initials for the National Indian Foundation (Brazil).

Genipapo *(gen ee papo)* The black dye or body paint taken from gum of the *genipa americana* tree.

Jacaranda *(jack ahr an dar)* The leaves of the jacaranda tree are used by Indians to relieve snakebites.

Jivaro *(hee vah ro)* A tribe.

Kreen-Akrore *(kren akror ay)* A tribe.

Maloca *(mal lo ka)* A large Indian hut shared by several families.

Manioc *(man ee ok)* The main root crop of the Amazon people.

Maracas *(ma rak ars)* A form of rattle made from gourds filled with pebbles.

Piranha *(pee ran a)* The so-called 'cannibal' fish much feared in Amazon water.

Pirarucu *(pee ra roo coo)* The largest scaled fish in the Amazon.

Shaman *(shah man)* A witchdoctor or medicine man.

Shipibo *(ship ee bo)* A tribe.

Shuar *(shoo ar)* A tribe.

Tanga *(tan gar)* A scanty covering, in ancient times made of ceramic. Today it is a tiny bikini.

Tipiti *(tee pee tee)* A tubular press made of plaited vine, for squeezing poison out of manioc.

Txukarramai *(ju cahra mei)* A tribe.

Urucu *(U roo coo)* A red dye taken from seeds of the *bixa orellana* shrub.

Yopo *(yop o)* A drug that stimulates hallucinations, used by shamans.

Picture acknowledgements

The illustrations in this book were supplied by the following: Douglas Botting 38; Camerapix Hutchison Library 18, 26 (lower), 27 (upper), 28, 33, 39, and the following pictures from W. Jesco von Puttkamer's collection 9, 19, 20, 21, 24, 25, 27 (lower), 32 (upper), 35, 36, 37, 41, 44; Goodyear Tyre & Rubber Co. 16 (right); Mary Evans Picture Library 10, 12, 14; South American Pictures *cover, frontispiece*, 6, 11 (Leimbach), 15 (lower), 16 (left), 23 (Leimbach), 26 (upper/Leimbach), 29 (both), 31, 32, (lower/Leimbach), 34 (Leimbach), 40, 42, 43, 45; Wayland Picture Library 7 (both), 8, 13, 15 (top), 16, 22, 30.

Index